Rainy Weather Days

by Pam Rosenberg

Children's Press®
A Division of Scholastic Inc.
New York Toronto London Auckland Sydney
Mexico City New Delhi Hong Kong
Danbury, Connecticut

These content vocabulary word builders are for grades 1–2.
Subject Consultants: Robert Van Winkle, Chief Meteorologist, WBBH, Fort Myers, Florida; and Jack Williams, Public Outreach Coordinator, American Meteorological Society, Boston, Massachusetts

Reading Consultant: Cecilia Minden-Cupp, PhD, Former Director of the Language and Literacy Program, Harvard Graduate School of Education, Cambridge, Massachusetts

Photographs © 2007: Corbis Images: 21 bottom (Stephen Frink), 5 top left, 9 (Julie Habel), 5 bottom right, 6 (Michael A. Keller/zefa), 20 bottom (Frans Lanting), 20 top (Robert Pickett), 5 top right, 16 (Jim Reed), 13 bottom, 23 bottom right (Royalty-Free), 23 bottom left (H. David Seawell), 21 top (David Woods); DK Images: 2, 15; Getty Images: back cover, 4 top, 12, 23 top right, (Brian Cosgrove/DK), cover (Marina Jefferson/Taxi), 13 top (Stephen Krasemann/Stone), 5 bottom left, 11 (Tim Sloan/AFP); Minden Pictures/Michael Durham: 21 center; Panos Pictures/Yann Mingard: 23 top left; Phototake/Ray Nelson: 4 bottom right, 17; Photri Inc./T. McCarthy: 19; Superstock, Inc./Lisette Le Bon: 1, 4 bottom left, 7.

Book Design: Simonsays Design!
Book Production: The Design Lab

Library of Congress Cataloging-in-Publication Data

Rosenberg, Pam.
  Rainy weather days / Pam Rosenberg.
    p. cm. — (Scholastic news nonfiction readers)
  Includes index.
  ISBN-10: 0-531-16769-0
  ISBN-13: 978-0-531-16769-4
  1. Rain and rainfall—Juvenile literature. I. Title. II. Series.
  QC924.7.T783 2007
  551.57'7—dc22   2006013305

1 2 3 4 5 6 7 8 9 10 R 16 15 14 13 12 11 10 09 08 07

CONTENTS

WORD HUNT

Look for these words as you read. They will be in **bold**.

clouds
(kloudz)

puddles
(**puhd**-uhlz)

rain gauge
(rayn gayj)

flowers
(**flou**-urz)

meteorologists
(mee-tee-ur-**ol**-uh-jists)

sleet
(sleet)

umbrella
(uhm-**brel**-uh)

5

Looks Like Rain

Splish! Splash! Grab your **umbrella** and boots. Let's go outside and find some **puddles**. It's going to be a rainy weather day!

umbrella

Boots keep your feet dry when you splash in puddles.

Spring can be a rainy season.

Springtime **flowers** need rain to grow. Sometimes people say that April showers bring May flowers!

Like all living things, these flowers need water to stay alive.

Spring isn't the only time it rains. It can rain in summer, fall, and winter, too.

Rain will turn icy if it is very cold outside. Icy rain is called **sleet**.

A sleet storm makes sidewalks and streets very slippery.

Raindrops come from **clouds**. A cloud is made of many tiny water droplets. The tiny droplets crash into each other. They make bigger drops. When the drops get too heavy they fall as rain.

clouds

Some clouds are rain clouds.

Other kinds of clouds can be seen on sunny days.

The smallest raindrops are the size of a tiny dot. Larger raindrops may be as big as a pea.

**size of
a small
raindrop**

**size of
a large
raindrop**

A raindrop changes shape as it falls.

A **rain gauge** is a long tube with a wide opening at the top. It is a tool that helps **meteorologists** measure how much rain falls during a storm.

meteorologists

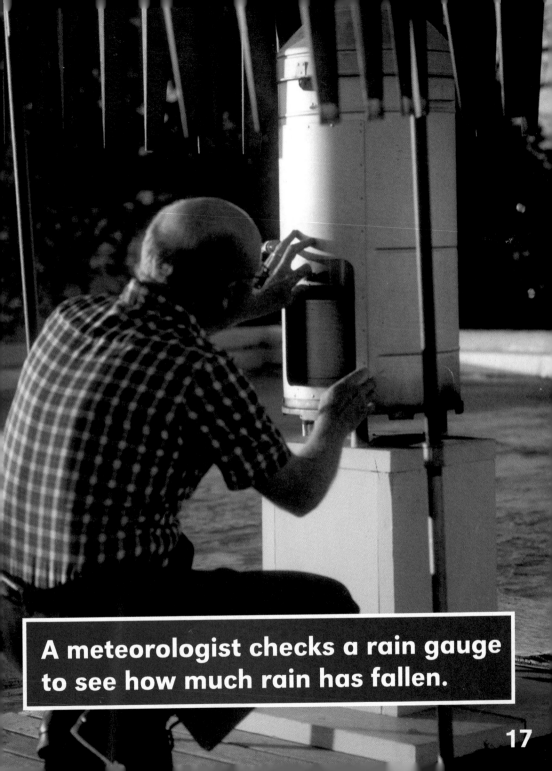

A meteorologist checks a rain gauge to see how much rain has fallen.

Rain fills up our lakes and rivers. It gives us water to drink and helps our food grow.

Rain helps make life on Earth possible. It makes splashing in puddles possible, too!

Sometimes it is fun
to play in the rain.

WHAT DO ANIMALS DO IN THE RAIN?

This worm came out of its hole.

This orangutan is catching raindrops.

This duck is taking a bath.

This tree frog is staying dry under a leaf.

Dolphins live in water. Do you think they notice when it rains?

YOUR NEW WORDS

clouds (kloudz) a large group of water droplets in the sky; clouds can be white or gray

flowers (**flou**-urz) the part of a plant that makes seeds or fruit

meteorologists (mee-tee-ur-**ol**-uh-jists) people who study Earth's weather

puddles (**puhd**-uhlz) a small pool of water on the ground

rain gauge (rayn gayj) a tool used to measure how much rain has fallen

sleet (sleet) rain that is partly frozen

umbrella (uhm-**brel**-uh) a frame with a cloth stretched over it that you hold over your head when it rains

WILL IT RAIN TODAY?

Watch for steady rain when you see these clouds.

Watch for light to heavy rain when you see these clouds.

Watch for a thunderstorm when you see these clouds.

You'll see these clouds on a sunny day.

INDEX

FIND OUT MORE

Book:

Bauer, Marion Dane. *Rain.* New York: Aladdin, 2004.

Website:

Weather Wiz Kids
http://www.weatherwizkids.com/Rain.ht

MEET THE AUTHOR:

Pam Rosenberg is an editor and author of children's books. She lives in Arlington Heights, Illinois, and likes to spend rainy weather days with her kids, Sarah and Jake, and her husband, Peter.